Money & Divorce: Costly Mistakes You Don't Want to Make

MONEY & DIVORCE: COSTLY MISTAKES YOU DON'T WANT TO MAKE

10 FINANCIAL MISTAKES
AND HOW TO AVOID THEM

RENEE W. SENES, CDFA
AND DAVID CHWALEK

Copyrighted Material

Money & Divorce: Costly Mistakes You Don't Want to Make

Copyright © 2017 by Renee W. Senes and David Chwalek.
All Rights Reserved.

No part of this publication may be reproduced, stored in a retrieval system or transmitted, in any form or by any means- electronic, mechanical, photocopying, recording or otherwise- without prior written permission from the publisher, except for the inclusion of brief quotations in a review.

ISBN-13: 978-1976382406
ISBN-10: 1976382408

Author photos courtesy of Lea Ferrante Photography

Acknowledgements

We gratefully acknowledge the many professional colleagues who have assisted us over the past several years. As the title of Chapter One states, "It takes a village." We have learned so much from you, and our clients benefit from our work together.

We are thankful to our clients who have done so much more than give us material for this book. You have challenged us to become more knowledgeable, creative and empathetic.

Finally, we thank our children for inspiring us. You continue to be a never-ending source of so much happiness and pride. We love you!

Table of Contents

Introduction

1. It Takes a Village   3
   Mistake #1: Failure to Seek Help

2. Show Me the Money!   13
   Mistake #2: Failure to Identify All the Assets

3. "I Owe, I Owe…"   21
   Mistake #3: Overlooking Debt and Credit Issues

   Renee's Story   29

4. The Nasty 'B' Word… Budget!   31
   Mistake #4: Failure to Analyze Income, Expenses and Liquidity

5. Not All Assets Are Created Equally   37
   Mistake # 5: Not Understanding Tax Issues

   David's Story   45

6. So, Who Gets to Keep the House?   49
   Mistake #6: Failure to Understand Decisions Regarding the House

7. Will You Still Need Me, Will You Still Feed Me?   59
   Mistake #7: Not Understanding the Rules about Retirement Plans and Social Security

8. Who's Got You Covered? 71
   Mistake #8: Overlooking Life and Health Insurance

9. Die and Endow a College or a Cat... but Not Your
   Ex-Spouse (With apologies to Alexander Pope) 75
   Mistake #9: Failure to Update Estate Planning
   Documents

10. It Ain't Over 'til It's Over 79
    Mistake #10: Failure to Follow through Once the
    Divorce is Final

Introduction

Senes and Chwalek is a full service investment advisory firm. We manage money for individuals and small businesses, help people save for retirement and plan for their children's college education. Over the years, working with people going through divorces has become a specialty of our firm. In addition to having both gone through a divorce ourselves, we are Certified Divorce Financial Analysts (CDFA) and use our background, expertise and experiences to help others avoid common mistakes we've seen time and time again.

We work with people in all stages of the divorce process: from thinking about it, or more often, *"Oh my god, my spouse wants a divorce"* (said in a panicked tone) to getting through it, taking the final steps and coming out whole on the other side. All too often we see signed settlements that leave one party in a financial bind. When we ask, "Why did you sign this?" the response is often something along the lines of "I just wanted it to be over."

When you're going through the pain and emotional battles of a divorce, it's easy to overlook financial issues that can hurt you long after any hard feelings have healed. You should expect that choices with huge financial implications will come at you with intense speed and they're probably not the sort of decisions you're used to making. There will be financial terminology you may not have heard before and you need to make certain you are very clear on how a particular asset will provide for you in the future. Not all assets are created equal.

Your best strategy before, during and after a divorce is knowledge. Complete and thorough knowledge about your finances: what you own, what you owe, what's coming in and what's going out. You need to be in control, familiar with your finances and ready to do some hands on management.

We are not an attorneys and this is not legal advice. We are not accountants and this is not tax advice. We urge all of you to consult with an attorney and an accountant if you are considering a divorce. If you have an attorney, or are in mediation, this is not intended to undo the decisions you've already hammered out.

In this book we'll look at 10 critical financial mistakes that are often made in divorce settlements and discuss how to avoid them. You'll gain an understanding of how issues around cash flow, liquidity, income taxes, capital gains, retirement account rules, insurance, debt and credit could impact your future well-being.

We'll offer real-life stories, expert opinions and practical solutions you can put in place.

Visit us at our website www.senesandchwalek.com. If you have a question you'd like us to address please send us an email or give us a call.

We wish you the best of luck.

Renee and David

Mistake #1: Failure to Seek Help

It takes a village

For many people, going through a divorce will be the single most stressful and traumatic period of their lives. Many will be forced to move out of their homes and see their children only at certain times on certain days. Others will find themselves struggling to make ends meet while caring for their children by themselves. Some people will lose old friends as these friends decide to align themselves with the spouse. They may feel ostracized by their former in-laws who blame the divorce solely on them. They find themselves the subject of neighborhood gossip, half-truths or outright lies. And their vision of the future now seems lonely and uncertain.

Everyone's divorce story is different, but they are rarely easy. During these difficult times it is imperative to have a support system. In this chapter, we'll discuss the types of people you need to have on your divorce support team.

<u>Attorney</u>

Probably the first professional you should engage is a family law attorney. These lawyers specialize in divorce as well as areas like child support and custody. If you didn't know it already, this will also be the time when you realize that getting divorced can be expensive. While legal fees can vary greatly based on a variety of factors including experience, reputation and location, it's not unusual for family law attorneys to charge $250 or more per hour for their services.

When hiring an attorney you will be asked to sign an engagement letter and pay a retainer. The engagement letter is the legal contract specifying the terms of your working relationship as well as the costs involved. The retainer is essentially a deposit or pre-payment of expected legal fees. If your actual expenses are less than the amount of the retainer, the difference should be returned to you. If your expenses exceed the amount of the retainer, you may be asked to pay another lump sum to cover future costs or you may simply be billed monthly for services rendered.

While many separated individuals will choose not to hire an attorney right away, if your situation is hostile or abusive, you should take this step *immediately*. Even if your situation is relatively calm and cooperative, you still might consider legal assistance if only to get a sense of your rights and what will be involved in the divorce process.

How do I find a good divorce lawyer?
In many ways, finding a good attorney is similar to finding a good dentist or hairdresser. Start by asking friends who have been through the process. Would they recommend their attorney? What did they like? What didn't they like? How responsive were they to calls and emails? Were they too aggressive? Not aggressive enough? What is their fee structure?

If you don't have any divorced friends or don't feel comfortable asking them, contact other professionals that you have been satisfied with and ask them for a referral. Lawyers are often a good source of referrals to other lawyers with different specialties. Financial advisors and accountants are also good sources because they often share clients with attorneys or have heard about them in professional networking groups.

Another good source is The Divorce Center, a Massachusetts non-profit, at www.thedivorcecenter.org.

Mediator

If your situation is amicable or if you and your spouse have committed to working together to reach a settlement that is mutually beneficial and/or in the best interests of the children, you might consider working with a divorce mediator. A mediator is often an attorney, but may also be a therapist or licensed social worker. A mediator does not represent either you or your spouse but is hired to work together with you both to develop and write the divorce agreement.

Mediation has become more popular over the past several years as people have begun looking for ways to save on legal costs during the divorce process. While hourly fees for a mediator may approach the range of costs for an attorney, you and your spouse would presumably be splitting the cost as opposed to each paying your own attorneys. If you and your spouse already have an idea or basic understanding of what you would like the settlement to look like, you may find that working with a mediator is a "more civilized" way to get divorced. If you know essentially what is most important to you and what you want- and your spouse knows too- then you may be able to save money with the mediation process.

Unfortunately, there are also people who choose to mediate *only* because they want to save on legal fees. If there is ongoing animosity, overly complex situations, dishonesty or a reluctance of one party to openly share financial documents, then mediation may not work for you.

Psychologist or therapist

For most of us, life is stressful enough even without going through a divorce. Add a divorce into the mix and you may have a real need to seek a professional with whom to discuss your feelings and problems.

David: Years ago, I thought only "crazy" people went to "shrinks." After beginning therapy and sharing my experiences with others, I was surprised at just how many people actually went to therapists. It seemed like everyone was doing it!

The emotions that people may feel during a divorce are numerous- shame, anger, guilt, resentment, sadness, relief, abandonment and hopelessness, to name a few. Eventually your divorce will become final, but you may still feel the lasting emotional effects for years to come. Before you can truly "move on," you need to come to terms with the psychological impact of the end of your marriage.

In the same way that you would go to a medical doctor if your body was injured or ill, you should consider going to a therapist to heal your mind and soul.

Most medical insurance now covers mental health and many providers accept insurance.

Certified Divorce Financial Analyst

In most divorce situations, financial implications and determining how to divide assets are of paramount concern. While many family law attorneys have varying degrees of financial acumen, it is important to remember that they are not, in most cases, financial experts. A Certified Divorce Financial Analyst (CDFA) is a financial advisor with special training in helping clients navigate the divorce process and reach an equitable financial agreement. Certified by the Institute for Divorce Financial Analysts, a CDFA has taken courses related to the various aspects of divorce and has passed a comprehensive final exam. They are required to complete continuing education each year and abide by the IDFA Code of Ethics. Although they are often well-versed in legal and tax matters, they do not intend to take the place of a lawyer or accountant.

A CDFA may be able to assist clients with determining the value of marital assets, creating a post-divorce budget, determining potential tax ramifications of selling the house or liquidating investments or retirement plans and much more. The CDFA often works in concert with your attorney and accountant and generally charges an hourly fee for consulting.

A CDFA may be able to help you with the following:
- What should we do with the house?
- Cash flow analysis and budgeting
- How much child support will I receive (or pay)?
- Buy versus rent analysis and mortgage options
- What are the tax implications of alimony?
- Review proposals set forth by attorneys or mediators
- How do we divide our 401(k) plans?
- Compare and contrast various settlement options
- Provide forecasts for future cash flow and net worth

In our practice, we have worked with hundreds of clients in all stages of the divorce process. Some have approached us who were simply *considering* a divorce. Others have the divorce agreement all written up and are just looking for a second opinion before they sign on the dotted line. Still others hire us post-divorce to help with budgeting, retirement planning and investment management.

Accountant

A good accountant will do more than simply file your tax return. In a divorce situation, he or she may prove to be invaluable in reviewing the tax ramifications of various aspects of the agreement. As we will discuss later in the book, alimony is taxable to the recipient and tax-deductible to the payer. Whether support is considered alimony or child support can have a significant impact on the financial situations of each party. In some cases, often depending on the respective tax brackets of the husband and wife, it actually makes sense for a higher amount of support to be paid but with a certain percentage to be characterized as alimony or family support.

When there are dependent children involved, a decision will need to be made as to which parent will be able to claim them as a dependent on their tax return. Sometimes the parents agree to alternate each year. Other times, they will determine which party would get a bigger tax benefit from the deduction in a given year.

While over-the-counter tax software has certainly become more robust- and complicated- in recent years, there is no substitute for a trained tax professional who understands the ins and outs of your personal circumstances.

Divorce coach or support group

Coaches have long been associated with athletics, but business and life coaches have become much more common and mainstream in the last decade. Would you believe there are actually divorce coaches too?

A divorce coach can provide you with guidance, support and resources to more effectively navigate your divorce.

While we had previously mentioned the importance of considering therapy, many of our clients have also benefitted from a divorce support group. Sharing your story with others who are empathetic with your situation can be a huge help. Even better is that you may stand to benefit from their experiences and learn what not to do!

Friends

While this hardly falls under the category of professional help, it's still help and you'll need it!

David: When I was first separated I found that many of my friends were sympathetic and probably really wanted to help. Unfortunately, most didn't know what to say or do. They hadn't been divorced and had no idea what I was going through. Like many things in life, you can't really understand what someone is going through until you've walked in their shoes.

Some of the best friends I had during my divorce were others who had been through it themselves. They understood why I wasn't "myself" lately. They could relate to my depression. They could understand my financial anxieties.

I think it's harder for men to reach out to other men about personal issues, so I was always (pleasantly) surprised when a few divorced guys I know would periodically call or email just to check in. "How you doing, buddy?" goes a long way sometimes. An offer to meet for coffee or a beer after work was appreciated more than they'll ever know.

So, I guess the point here is to find or keep close to supportive friends. Sometimes you just need someone to talk to or someone to vent to. Steer clear of those that are just looking for the latest dirt from your divorce proceedings. It's important to surround yourself with positive people. They'll be the wind for your sails as you approach your new life.

<u>Your To Do List</u>:

1. Contact three attorneys or mediators and set up informational meetings
2. Find a local support group and attend a meeting

Mistake #2: Failure to Identify and Protect All Assets

Show me the money!

Do you know your credit score or the details of your Social Security report? Can you find the deed to your house, mortgage, life insurance policies, car title, car insurance policies, tax returns for the past 5 years, brokerage and bank statements for the past year? Do you know what your spouse earns or how much is going into a 401k plan annually?

Getting divorced is often a wake-up call when it comes to finding out what you know and don't know about your family finances.

In many marriages, there is one spouse who handles the finances. This person may pay the monthly bills, keep track of and/or manage the investments and file the tax returns. If you are that person in your marriage, then you are probably ahead of the game and have a decent understanding of your family's financial situation. If that person is *not* you, then you have some work to do to get up to speed.

Navigating a divorce is much like the Boy Scout motto, *"Be prepared."* In order to effectively enter into mediation, or understand the terms of a settlement offer proposed by your attorney, you need to know 4 basic things ahead of time:

1. What you own
2. What you owe
3. What's coming in
4. What's going out

In this chapter, we'll focus on **What You Own**.

We've seen many divorce settlements where it seems that one party is short-changed because they simply didn't identify and understand the nature of their marital assets.

What is an asset? An asset is anything that you *own*. (Anything you *owe* is called a liability- we'll get to those later.) Assets include cash, bank accounts, investments and retirement accounts, real estate, cars and other valuables such as jewelry, art and collectibles.

Before you begin listing your assets, you'll want to clear off a workspace and gather every financial document you can find. Other helpful supplies include pencils or pens, highlighters, a 3-ring binder, hole punch and index divider. (Renee finds that a box of cookies really helps, too.)

What do you need to gather?

- Tax returns: get copies of at least a few years of federal tax returns
- Bank statements: if you don't have paper statements, these can usually be obtained at your bank's website or by contacting your bank
- Investment statements: again, these can generally be found online if you don't have paper copies
- Retirement plan statements: 401(k), pensions, IRAs, etc.

- Credit card statements
- Real estate deeds: in Massachusetts, these can be found online
- Pay stubs: for you and your spouse

<u>What are you looking for?</u>

Tax returns are a good first place to start. The first page shows reported income- not just from a job, but from interest and dividends from bank or investment accounts, rental real estate income, self-employment and profits (or losses) from the sale of real estate or investments. In addition, if you or your spouse took money out of a retirement account like an IRA or 401(k) plan, it will show up here. On page 2, if a refund is due, this is a marital asset.

Schedule A would show deductions for gambling losses being claimed- gambling *winnings* may be hidden by the losses.

On Schedule B of the tax return, any account that earned interest or dividends will appear here. Were you aware of these? Make sure you find the statements for the accounts listed. Schedule B does not state how much money was in the accounts, only how much money was generated from interest or dividends. Note: retirement accounts often pay dividends and interest, but they will **not** appear on Schedule B because those earnings are not taxable.

Schedule D of the tax return shows the profits (known as capital gains) and losses (capital losses) resulting from the sale of an investment such as a stock, mutual fund or real estate. (Again, gains or losses from retirement plans will not show up here.) The first reason to check out Schedule

D is simply to identify investments that you may or may not have known about. The second reason is to determine if your spouse has sold investments and taken the money. It should be noted that in 90% of the cases we work with, selling securities is absolutely normal and quite routine. Just because you notice a capital gain, it doesn't mean your spouse was doing something behind your back. Stocks and mutual funds are often sold in investment accounts and then the proceeds are reinvested into different stocks or mutual funds. Once you see that a transaction or transactions have occurred, you'll want to check the statements to see what happened to the proceeds.

How can losses be an asset?
When an investment is sold at a loss, it is either a long-term loss or short-term loss. Short-term losses involve sales that were made in less than 12 months after the investment was purchased and result in receiving proceeds less than the original purchase price. Long-term losses involve investments that were held for more than one year and then sold at a loss. Capital losses are often helpful because they can be used to offset capital gains and thereby reduce your tax liability. Losses can be claimed up to the extent that you have gains plus an additional $3,000 per year. For example, it you have capital gains of $4,000 in a given year and $12,000 in losses, you can offset the $4,000 in gains with $4,000 in losses and take another $3,000 in losses. You nullify any potential tax liability on the gain and actually get a tax deduction for the extra $3,000 in losses. But what happens to that extra $5,000 in losses we weren't able to "use" this year? Capital losses can be carried forward for use in future years! So, if, for example, you have $5,000 in gains next year, you can offset them with the $5,000 in losses from last year.

Carry-forward capital losses are considered an asset! If you have carry-forward losses, be sure to account for these in your divorce agreement.

Reviewing bank account and credit card statements can be helpful to make sure there weren't any unusual purchases or withdrawals that you weren't aware of. (You'll need these statements again when we discuss expenses and budgeting.)

Pay stubs contain a wealth of useful information. In addition to showing salary, overtime, bonuses and commissions, you'll find information about the cost of benefits and contributions to retirement plans. Is life insurance being paid for through payroll deduction? How much is going into the 401(k) plan each week? Are earnings being direct deposited into an account I didn't know about?

Finally, don't forget about your children's savings or college accounts. We'll again point out that there is hardly ever any funny business going on with these accounts. There is one story, however, of a husband who funded his children's 529 college savings accounts with the intent of hiding money from his wife. By stashing $260,000 into these accounts during the divorce, he figured that these were assets that could not be touched by his wife. Sadly for him, a judge ruled that half the money was hers. You can't shelter money in a divorce by giving it to your kids.

Valuing your assets

At this point we want to list all our marital assets and their current values. Some assets like stocks change in value every day, so you'll need to pick a date and value all your assets as of that date. Remember, this is just a snapshot in time.

Important note: List all assets, regardless of whose name they are registered in. In other words, your wife's work 401(k) is still considered a marital asset.

Bank accounts- These are the easiest. Just use the current balance as of the day you choose.

Retirement accounts- For most retirement plans, this is as simple as recording the market value as of a certain date. Retirements accounts like these include 401(k) plans, 403(b) plans, IRAs, Roth IRAs, SIMPLE IRAs, SEPs and Single Ks (401k for self-employed). Valuing traditional pension plans is a little more difficult. First, you'll need to contact your employer for the annual benefit of the pension if you retire at the earliest age possible. If you have a financial calculator, you can probably figure out the present value of your future pension payments by yourself. If not, your financial professional should be able to help.

Securities accounts- These would be non-retirement investment accounts. Typical securities include stocks, bonds, mutual funds and real estate investment trusts. Check your account statements or call your advisor for current market values. While you're at it, make sure you get the cost basis of the securities you own. The cost basis is the original cost of the security adjusted for commissions, dividends and stock splits. Until the last few years, financial organizations were not required to keep track of basis. Your cost basis may be listed right on your account statements especially if you own a brokerage account. If not, you may need to contact your advisor or firm for assistance. We'll discuss the importance of knowing cost basis later in Chapter 5.

Real estate- Before agreeing to a property settlement, you'll want to have an appraisal of your house done by a local realtor. In the meantime, you can get a pretty reasonable estimate of your home's value at www.zillow.com. It may not be 100% accurate or take into account special features of your house or neighborhood, but it's a good starting point. For rental properties, an appraisal is recommended. Investment real estate tends to be valued differently than residential property.

Automobiles- You may not have any idea what your cars are worth, but there are a few good online tools to help get a good estimate of market value. Try www.kbb.com (Kelley Blue Book) or www.edmunds.com. You'll need to know the year, make and model as well as the mileage and what trim the car is (i.e. Pathfinder ES, Pathfinder LS, etc.).

Jewelry, art, Oriental rugs, etc. - If you have a fair amount of these, you will definitely want to get an appraisal before beginning negotiations with your spouse. For now, you might check your home insurance policies. If any of these items are particularly valuable, you may have scheduled them on your policy, which would have required an appraisal.

Your To Do List:

1. Obtain 3 years of tax returns. If not in your personal records or with your accountant, they are available from the IRS by using IRS Tax Form 4506 Request for Copy of Tax Return. There is a $50 fee for each return that you request and it may take up to 75 days to process your request.
2. Organize! Getting divorced involves a lot of paperwork. Buy a portable file folder/carrying case from an office supply store. You can bring it to your meetings and it has the added advantage of being able to be put away when not needed so your divorce doesn't take over your dining room table, kitchen counter and daily life.

Mistake #3: Failure to Resolve Debt and Credit Rating Issues

"I Owe, I Owe"

Nothing is worse than starting out a new life with bad credit. You're going to need to be able to borrow money.

1st: Obtain a copy of your credit report. This will identify all joint accounts, accounts you may not have been aware of, and any potential credit problems. Your credit history is free every year on www.annualcreditreport.com. There are 3 companies: Experian, Transunion and Equifax. Look at your credit history to make sure the information is correct. If not, correct any errors in writing. You can keep track of your credit all year by a simple method: tomorrow, order your credit report from Experian. Wait 4 months and order your credit report from Transunion. In another 4 order it from Equifax and by this time next year you'll be ready to start over again with Experian. Then get your own credit card (retail, gas). This will help to create an individual credit history. When you are on your own, you will have a better chance qualifying for loans, mortgages and credit cards. These are all important considerations after a divorce.

2nd: If possible, pay off and close all joint accounts and open new accounts in your own name. Creditors don't care how a separation agreement divides responsibility for joint debt (joint credit cards, auto loans etc.). Each person is liable for the full amount of debt until the balance is paid. If your spouse files for bankruptcy the creditor will look to you for payment.

3rd: Regarding income tax debt, even if the divorce is final, you may not be exempt from future tax liability. For 3 years after the divorce, the IRS can perform a random audit of a divorced couple's joint tax return. If it has good cause, the IRS can question a joint return for 7 years. To avoid any potential problems down the road, your divorce agreement should have provisions that spell out what happens if any additional penalties, interest or taxes are found as well as where the funds come from to pay for any expenses associated with an audit.

Remember that a divorce divides not only assets but debt. If paying off marital debt is not possible, you will need to come to some resolution about which party is responsible for which debt. And herein lies a world of misunderstanding.

Let's look at a typical divorce agreement covering an automobile. While married, the couple purchased, and financed, a 2016 Honda. It was always considered the "wife's car" and she will receive it as part of the divorce settlement. Because there is still an outstanding loan on the vehicle, title to the car cannot be transferred into her name alone yet.

> *The parties agree as follows: The wife shall retain the 2016 Honda for her use. The Wife shall be responsible for all costs, including but not limited to any outstanding loan payments, maintenance, insurance, and excise. After the fulfillment of the loan, the Husband shall transfer all his right, title and interest to the wife. The Wife shall indemnify and hold harmless the Husband for any issues that arise regarding this automobile.*

What has happened?
- The wife has sole use of the car and is responsible for all costs.
- The husband's name is still on the car title and the car loan.

What could happen?
- The wife, financially strapped, stops paying the loan.
- The car gets repossessed.
- The bank or finance company holding the auto loan comes after the husband for payment.

Can the bank do this? Yes!

But what about the wife's promise to hold harmless and indemnify the Husband? Here's the misunderstanding: the promise is binding only between the husband and the wife. It does not bind the loan company. The Husband, in our example, is obligated to pay the debt. He can always sue his former wife, but now we're talking about hiring an attorney, going to court, getting a judgment — what a headache!

We're not saying you should never do this. Sometimes there are no alternatives. Just be certain that you fully understand what you've agreed to. If your name is still on the debt instrument — car loan, school loan, mortgage, credit card — you are still liable regardless of what the divorce agreement may say. As long as you realize that, you're okay to go ahead and sign.

Maintaining good credit has taken on greater importance now than ever before. A good credit score can help you get better interest rates and terms on mortgages and car loans. Insurance companies also look at your credit now and a bad score could have you paying a higher premium. Many landlords and property managers will check your credit before agreeing to rent you an apartment. And some employers run credit checks and- fair or not- view your score as a potential snapshot of your reliability and integrity.

Here are a few tips to improve your credit score:
- Ideally, try to keep your balances below 10% of your available credit.
- It's better to spread your balances evenly over a few credit cards than all on one.
- Being over 70% of your credit limit on any card is detrimental to your score.
- Don't close cards with zero balances even if you don't use them. Closing them reduces your available credit and thus hurts your ratio of credit used to credit available.

Let's look at another case. Mark and Jane are in their 40's – too young to access retirement money without a 10% early withdrawal penalty. How do you get divorced when your house is underwater, and you have significant debt?

Asset	Mark	Jane	Joint	
Real Property				
value: 409,000			(77,000)	
mtg: 426,000				
heloc: 60,000				
Total Real Property	0	0	(77,000)	(77,000)
Non-Retirement Assets				
Total Non-Retirement Assets	0	0	0	0
Retirement Assets				
401k	116,000	25,000		
value: 140,000				
loan: 24,000				
Total Retirement Assets	116,000	25,000		141,000
Debt				
Car			(18,000)	
Credit cards			(42,000)	
Student loans			(32,000)	
Total Debt			(92,000)	(92,000)
TOTAL	116,000	25,000	(169,000)	(28,000)

The mediated suggestion was that Mark use his 401k to transfer $92,000 to Jane to pay off the debt. This is allowable, and avoids the 10% penalty for early withdrawal, when coming from a QDRO (see retirement chapter).

There are 2 problems with this solution:

1. The 401k plan will automatically withhold 20% of the distribution for taxes. This means Jane receives $73,600 which is not sufficient to cover the debt. To cover the debt they would have to transfer $115,000.
2. The $92,000 is taxable income to Jane and, when added to her employment income for the year, bumps her into the next tax bracket.

What might be an alternative?

1. Mark can borrow up to $50,000 from his 401k. This means he can borrow an additional $26,000 with no tax consequences. He uses that to pay off some of the debt. The debt now reduces to $66,000 ($92,000 – $26,000 = $66,000)
2. Jane can trade in her 5 year old SUV and buy a smaller, less expensive car. There will be a loan but at least she'll have a new car. The debt now reduces to $48,000 ($66,000 – $18,000 = $48,000)
3. Mark now has $90,000 in his 401K ($140,000 – $50,000 loan = $90,000). He transfers $60,000 to Jane. $12,000 (20%) gets automatically withheld for taxes and $48,000 pays off their debt.

The advantages:

1. Mark's 401k loan is repaid through payroll deductions. Essentially he pays himself back.
2. Jane has a new car, in her own name, and Mark is no longer obligated on the debt.
3. Jane's income taxes are somewhat reduced by the addition of only $60,000 to her income instead of $92,000.

We would be remiss if we did not insert a comment on bankruptcy. While no likes to consider filing for bankruptcy, sometimes it's the only viable option and may be the safest way to navigate your divorce.

<u>Your To Do List</u>:

1. Check your credit score
2. Check your spouse's credit score
3. Stop using joint credit cards whenever possible
4. Obtain a credit card solely in your own name
5. Understand the implications of your agreement regarding debt division and what future obligation you may have to pay the debt

Renee's Story

Approaching the summer of 2002, I began contemplating a romantic trip to Paris for my upcoming 50th birthday. My husband was contemplating something entirely different – divorce. Consequently, just shy of my 50th birthday, I found myself on what I call the "receiving end" of a divorce.

Even though I was the one in our family who paid the bills and managed- and still manage- the retirement plan for my ex-husband's company, I panicked. Part of the panic was emotional: I was 50, with two young children- *who would want me? I'd be alone for the rest of my life!* But a big part of the panic was financial: how would I support myself, would I get alimony, child support, could I refinance the house, what about medical insurance, would I ever be able to retire?

We chose to mediate. While I truly liked our mediator and have clients who use him, I found that he didn't offer a lot of direction. If I hadn't known my bottom line going into the mediation I would have been in trouble. I see the same thing with clients who hire an attorney. They have a settlement but they have no understanding of what that settlement means in practical terms – will I be able to buy a house or condo, can I cover my expenses, what happens when my daughter needs braces?

In the ensuing years, I've met numerous men and women struggling with the fallout from their divorce: changes in finances, lifestyle, community and friendships. Every client has a story and is free to share as much or as little as comfort allows. I share parts of my story as it seems appropriate and helpful. There is never any judgment being made on my part. I do what I do because I've sat on their side of the table. I know what it's like to question the decisions that have been made over the many years of a marriage.

I became a Certified Divorce Financial Analyst specifically to help my clients deal with these issues. I am trained to assist clients to gather and compile financial information, prepare scenarios of possible settlements, and help to understand the upside and downside of the various options. I will prepare a marital balance sheet, a cash flow forecast, and a net worth forecast. These will help clients to look at the implications of how different asset divisions will impact cash flow and overall financial health over time. Once the settlement is finalized, I will work with my client to invest for their future.

More recently I trained as a mediator. The mediation training was intense and eye opening bringing up emotional issues I thought were long resolved. It gave me a much clearer understanding of the lifelong challenge of divorce. While I don't mediate cases, I will act as a financial neutral helping both parties to understand how their financial decisions will shape their lives and those of their children.

My goal, always, is to educate my clients to understand what they own and to enable them to manage their finances so they can be financially independent, as well as competent and comfortable working with money.

Mistake #4: Failure to Analyze Income, Expenses and Liquidity

The Nasty 'B' Word... Budget!

Start by making a list of everything you own: house, car, brokerage accounts, life insurance, retirement accounts and their value. Use the internet to help (www.kbb.com, www.zillow.com), your real estate tax bill, etc. This is the time to open those brokerage and 401k statements that you've been avoiding. Not looking is not going to help. Add these all up. The value of everything you own is called your assets.

Then, make a list of everything you owe: mortgage, car loan, credit card debt, school loans and their value as well. These are your liabilities.

The difference between what you own and what you owe is your Net Worth.

Next, begin tracking all of your monthly income and expenses. Use a notebook, sheets of paper, one credit card, Quicken, QuickBooks, or web sites such www.mint.com and www.yodlee.com.

The difference between your income and your expenses is your cash flow, which is just a fancy name for – you guessed it – your budget.

It's easy to underestimate or omit expenses when you produce your initial budget for temporary maintenance, and then later on in the divorce process find yourself unable to pay bills. Also consider your income on an after tax basis. Remember: child support is taxable to the person paying it but not taxable to the person receiving it, while alimony is taxable to the person receiving it and tax deductible to the person paying it. Consider which spouse could best benefit when awarding the right to future tax deductions and credits relating to the couple's children.

Take a good hard look at your expenses versus liquid assets and income.

Liquidity refers to the ability to access the cash value of an asset. For example, a bank savings account is highly liquid, because you can simply withdraw funds when you need them. An antique automobile, however, is nearly illiquid because it is very difficult to quickly sell this asset to access the actual cash value.

Often in a divorce settlement, one party will receive mostly illiquid assets, including the home, while the other party receives liquid assets such as retirement plans or brokerage accounts. This may appear to be equitable if they are of approximately the same value. However, the challenge lies in cash flow. How will you pay the bills if your major asset, the home, is illiquid?

Which leads us to another common mistake - the failure to budget based on your new lifestyle. One indisputable fact of divorce is that two households cost more to operate than one, but income is unchanged. A post-divorce lifestyle may look very different than the one you had while married. Renee found herself eating out much more often in order to be with friends.

HIRED HELP- Once there are no longer two of you around, you may have to hire others for everything from yard maintenance and home repair to babysitting. This cost ought to be part of your budget — and negotiations.

TEENAGERS- If you have joint custody of your children, you may end up buying computers, clothes and other items for their second residence. What many couples don't anticipate or budget for if their children are small, however, are the extra costs of the teenage years: prom expenses, cheerleading, sports gear, cars and car insurance, allowance and college visits and applications. The actual cost of college is a big one, too. And don't forget cell phones.

FUTURE LEGAL COSTS- Even after tallying up all of the above, you still have to consider that years later, your spouse may come after you for more money or try to pay less after a job loss. Then you're liable for more in legal bills. While you may not want to earmark emergency funds just for that, the larger point is this: Long after you move on emotionally, divorce may haunt you financially.

Before you consider a settlement that has very little liquidity, be sure that you will have enough cash flow throughout the years to handle your living expenses. You need to project several years into the future and determine if you'll have enough resources to support your current lifestyle as well as your retirement years. This analysis should be completed prior to a settlement. If it is determined that you will be unable to maintain your lifestyle with the proposed offer, you may have established a good case to request more assets, alimony or child support.

Let's look at a case where the wife chose to take the house.

Asset	Husband	Net Husband	Wife	Net Wife		
Real Property						
House			385,000	385,000		
value: 525,000						
mtg: 140,000						
Total Real Property			385,000			
Non-Qualified Assets						
Brokerage account	117,566	93,700				
Brokerage account	1,826	1,455				
QDRO 401k		40,407	88,340	30,000		1
Total Non-Qualified Assets	119,392	135,562	88,340	30,000		

Qualified Assets					
Roth	17,587	17,587			
IRA	116,299	92,690			
401k - former employer	88,340	0			
401k - former employer	197,998	157,804			
Current 401k	70,116	55,882			
Roth			32,868	32,868	
YYZ IRA			37,249	29,687	
TDA			47,203	37,621	
Total Qualified Assets	402,000	323,963	95,752	100,176	
Car	1,000				
Car			10,000		
Total Vehicles	1,000	1,000	10,000	10,000	
TOTAL	522,392	460,525	600,660	525,176	1,123,052
Total Estate	46.5%		53.48%		
Total Estate Net of Taxes		46.72%		53.28%	985,701

The purpose of the QDRO will be to free up cash without incurring a 10% penalty for early withdrawal under age 59 1/2. This will enable husband to have sufficient cash for a down payment. The 401k custodian will automatically withhold 20% to pay Federal taxes. This may be refunded upon the filing of a tax return if it is an overpayment.

*The net from the QDRO will be 70,407. From this, wife will receive $30,000 and husband will receive $40,407.

Estimated combined Federal and State Tax rate at 20.30% - NOTE 2016 Massachusetts rate is now 5.10%

Tax basis on non-retirement assets is calculated as capital gains

One of the first things you may notice is that she has very little cash. This means that she is solely dependent on her own job related income and any child support or alimony that she receives. There is nothing available for emergency back-up. This is an example of not taking liquidity into account when dividing assets.

<u>Your To Do List</u>:

1. Compile a list of your assets and liabilities
2. Make a comprehensive list of your expected expenses going forward

Mistake #5: Not Understanding Tax Issues

Not All Assets are Created Equally

The effect on your settlement of various taxes can be very costly if not addressed thoroughly. Capital gains, income tax, and alimony are just a few of the areas that may be impacted.

Capital gains taxes need to be analyzed when property is being divided. Capital gains refer to the fair market value of an asset minus its cost. For example, if you paid $5 for a share of stock and it is now worth $25, you have a capital gain of $20. This applies to other assets such as real estate (including your home), mutual fund accounts and just about any investment that has appreciated in value.

Be very careful that the property you are receiving in a settlement does not have large capital gains as compared with your ex-spouse's property.

As an example, you may be offered an investment account worth $150,000, but the cost basis is only $50,000. That means there is a gain of $100,000 that you must pay- at minimum- long-term capital gains tax (15%) on. There could possibly be short-term gains as well, which are taxed at your own marginal tax rate.

Let's take a look at another example. Bob and Ellen are divorcing and have the following assets totaling $640,000:

- Vacation cottage in Maine worth $150,000
- Brokerage account worth $170,000

- Bank accounts worth $280,000 (mostly proceeds from selling their marital home)
- Apartment furnishings valued at $20,000
- Car valued at $20,000

They agreed that Bob would keep the vacation cottage and brokerage account, while Ellen would get the bank accounts, furnishings and car.

At first glance, it would appear to be an equitable division of assets. Each of them ends up with $320,000 worth of assets- exactly one half.

Knowing a little more about the assets- and understanding potential tax liabilities- we see that this arrangement may not be fair at all.

You see, most of the investments in the brokerage account were purchased several years ago, but the biggest winner in the portfolio is a stock that has soared 45% since they bought it just 8 months ago. Here is a breakdown of the portfolio:

Stock	Cost	Current value	Gain/loss	Long/short term
APPL	12,000	37,500	25,500	Long
XOM	11,000	31,000	20,000	Long
IBM	14,000	28,000	14,000	Long
PFE	18,000	30,000	12,000	Long
XIX	30,000	43,500	13,500	Short

If Bob decides to sell the stocks- which he probably will because he doesn't have any liquid assets- he will have to pay capital gains taxes. The stocks that he's owned for a long time have *long-term* gains because they've been held for over 12 months. The gains on his long-term stocks (Apple, ExxonMobil, IBM and Pfizer) total $71,500. As long-term gains, they'll be taxed at a 15% rate, so he'll owe $10,725.

The gain on XIX is considered *short-term*, because it's been owned for less than 12 months. The $13,500 gain will be taxed at Bob's ordinary income tax rate (in this case, we'll assume 28%), so he'll pay $3,780.

So Bob's $170,000 asset is really worth only $155,495 after paying taxes.

For Bob, it gets worse. He thought he'd end up living in the vacation cottage, but after only a few winter months in Maine, he found it isolated and pretty depressing. He decided to sell it.

After paying a sales commission and other closing costs, he ended up with $140,000 from the sale. But this is before taxes… Because the cottage was Bob's primary residence for only a short time (less than 2 of the last 5 years), the gain from the sale is treated as an investment gain. Bob and Ellen bought the cottage 22 years ago- well before the real estate boom- for $20,000. Since Bob cleared $140,000 from the sale and the cost basis is only $20,000, he has a long-term capital gain of $120,000. At a 15% rate, he'll owe $18,000 in taxes.

Because Ellen ended up with cash, furniture and the car, she has no tax liability at all.

Let's now take another look at this supposed equitable division:

Asset	Value	Ellen's ½	Bob's ½	Ellen's net proceeds	Bob's net proceeds
Vacation cottage	150,000		150,000		150,000
					Basis 20,000
					Cap gain 120,000
					Tax 18,000
					Sales Costs 10,000
					Net 122,000
Brokerage account	170,000		170,000		**After Tax 155,495**
Bank accounts	280,000	280,000		280,000	
Apartment furnishings	20,000	20,000		20,000	
Car	20,000	20,000		20,000	
TOTAL	640,000	320,000	320,000	320,000	277,495

As it turns out, poor Bob ends up with $42,505 less than Ellen. Had he taken taxes into account during the negotiation process, he never would have agreed to the proposed division of assets.

Clearly, income taxes need to be analyzed when property is being divided. Retirement plans will be discussed in greater detail in Mistake # 7. Basically, most retirement plans are funded pre-tax. This means that when you take the money out you will owe ordinary income tax on the money at both the federal and state level based on your then current tax bracket.

Taxes on the sale of your house have special rules. The Tax Relief Act of 1997 changed the tax rules regarding the sale of your principal residence. The rules are:

> 1. Each individual can exclude $250,000 from capital gains.
>
> 2. Married couples can therefore exclude $500,000.
>
> 3. The property you're selling must be your principal residence -this is accomplished when you meet the IRS use and ownership tests- you own and live in the home for two out of the five years before the sale.
>
> 4. You can do this once every two years.

There are also special rules that relate to divorce governing the use period and the ownership period that assist with taking advantage of the capital gains exclusion even if one spouse is no longer living in the marital home.

Options for the house:

1. Sell and Divide the Equity while still married ($500,000 exclusion)

2. Joint Ownership
One spouse remains in jointly owned house pursuant to the separation agreement or divorce decree and sells at the end of the agreed upon period (i.e. child graduates from high school). ½ of the proceeds go to the non-resident spouse who can still use the $250,000 exclusion for a combined total of $500,000.

3. One Spouse Takes the House Solely
Look at tax consequences! You might have planned to stay but circumstances or finances changed your plans. You now have only your own 250,000 exclusion.

Renee: As part of my settlement, I chose to keep my house and buy my husband out by refinancing. In those years mortgage money was easy to obtain and I never thought twice about the financial ramifications of taking on a big house on my own. When I finally do choose to sell, all closing costs and capital gains taxes will be solely my responsibility. Today, if I were my own client, I'd advise myself not to do that.

Even for financially savvy people, understanding all of the impacts of taxes can be daunting.

Your To Do List:

1. Make sure you have the cost basis information for any securities accounts
2. Understand the potential tax ramifications of selling your house

David's Story

Growing up in a small, rural town in northeast Connecticut in the 1970's and 80's, hardly anyone I knew ever got divorced. My parents were married for over forty years. My friends all had moms and dads who lived together. Every now and then, you'd hear about someone getting divorced and it was almost newsworthy.

As I got older, graduated from college and began a career in financial planning, I'd meet clients who were divorced and, in some cases, met couples who were married but later ended up getting divorced. As a young professional entering the dawn of the 21st century, I began to see that divorce was actually pretty common. Yes, I know, we've all heard the statistics- nearly 1 in 2 marriages end in divorce, or something like that. Even then, I never anticipated that divorce would someday have such a profound effect on my business- and my life.

In 2003, I began working with a business coach. One of my initial assignments was to break down and analyze my clientele and look for commonalities. The most eye-opening part of this exercise for me was compiling a list of my 20 biggest clients. What did they have in common? Did they have similar occupations or hobbies? Were they men or women? Did they live in the same town? As it turned out, 13 of my top 20 clients were divorced. I never planned it that way. It certainly wasn't part of my business plan to work with predominantly divorced people. In fact, of those 13, only one came to me specifically because she was getting divorced and needed some financial guidance. I guess it just happened, but I thought it was worth exploring further.

As I continued working with my coach, we would brainstorm about ways to market my practice and target specific demographic groups. I wondered if divorced people were actually a target market. In further analyzing my clientele, it became apparent that my divorced clients had different needs and concerns than my married clients. In many cases, I found that one spouse had handled the family finances while one was often less experienced with financial matters. They needed help from someone like me.

Around this time, I discovered the Institute for Divorce Financial Analysts (www.instituteDFA.com). The Institute offered training and support for financial professionals working in this arena and resources for those going through a divorce. I began studying and learning more about the legal, tax and financial ramifications of divorce and, in 2004, I earned my Certified Divorce Financial Analyst (CDFA) designation. I felt I must be ready to become a divorce financial planning specialist!

For the next few years, I continued marketing my practice just as I had before and picked up a few more divorced clients along the way. I still wasn't specifically targeting them, but it was more luck of the draw.

Then in 2008, I found myself separated from my wife. My world was turned upside down. I was away from my three young children. Instead of living in a charming colonial within walking distance of my office in beautiful Concord, Massachusetts, I was looking for a small apartment that I could barely afford. I felt embarrassed, ashamed and scared. No one ever thinks it will happen to them, but here I was… and it was happening to me.

As our separation eventually led to divorce, financial matters took center stage. What will happen to the house? How much support will I be paying? Despite my experience in personal finance and helping other people deal with their divorces, I felt very much a novice. I never could have imagined the emotional toll that comes with going through a divorce. Simple tasks became nearly impossible to complete. Every day was miserable and seemed to drag on forever. I couldn't believe what my life had become, and I wouldn't wish my experiences on my worst enemy.

While my ex-wife and I have been able to maintain a good working relationship with regard to the children, we have had more than our share of arguments and disagreements, almost all of them over money. I know we both wish that all of the money spent on attorneys over the last few years could have been put to better use. My divorce was painful- emotionally and financially. If you've never been through it, count your blessings.

Somehow, my own personal misfortune and struggles with divorce have helped me to discover the missing aspect of my professional dealings with people going through divorce. I now had empathy. As an objective third party, I could always understand the dollars and cents part. Now, I could understand the emotional part. I've been there. I know how hard it is.

As I write this, it's been nearly eight years since my divorce was final. I'm still not completely healed, but I'm moving in the right direction. My children are wonderful and I'm fortunate that I see them often. My relationship with my ex-wife, while still a work in progress, is getting better.

No one ever plans to get divorced. Worlds are turned upside down and lives are forever changed. I've worked in the divorce financial planning area for several years now and have many personal experiences to draw from, as well. It is my hope that I can help you survive your divorce and avoid the mistakes that I've seen others make. We're in a club that no one wants to join. But, now that we're here, we're all pulling for each other. I made it. You will too.

Mistake #6: Failure to Understand Decisions Regarding the House

"So, Who Gets to Keep the House?"

We could write chapters about just this one topic – and before we're done, we just might. Renee kept her house. David's ex-wife kept their house. We'll bring you different personal perspectives as well as financial and tax advice.

> **Renee's House**
> My ex and I finally separated in the winter of 2003. My children were 17 and 12. They had both been born in our town, lived here all their lives, gone to school here and made good friends in our small community – as had I. At the time, our town had no apartments, no condominiums and I reasoned that "the devil I knew" (my house) was better than "the devil I didn't" (downsizing into a smaller or fixer up house). I decided I would buy my ex out and stay until my son, the 12 year old, finished high school. Mortgage money was easily obtainable in those days. Even though I was self-employed and working part time I was able to get a no asset, no income verification mortgage in very short order and the house was mine- along with all the headaches and repairs I hadn't factored in to ownership.
>
> In the years since I've owned my house I've had: 2 major lightning strikes that took out my well pump, garage doors and all electric appliances; ice dams that, upon melting, rained into the downstairs bathroom and required major reconstruction; 2 major ice storms that left me without

> power for 8 and 5 days each (not only no lights and no heat but no water and no toilets that flush – UGH!) and severe tree damage. Then there are all the day to day house issues: mowing, plowing, painting, leaking toilets, the light bulbs on the cathedral ceiling I can't reach because I'm not big enough to carry the extension ladder all by myself. And lastly, I'm closing in on the 35 year mark with this house and there are still several things that need replacement or updating- the kitchen, the bathrooms, carpeting... the list goes on.
>
> The ongoing cost of keeping this house has been extraordinary and was not something I ever considered when I originally planned to keep it. However, I readily admit, my home has been a source of great comfort, security and pleasure. The 12 year old is now 25, the real estate down turn intervened and I'm still here. Almost forgot- the back deck needs replacing!

Let's look at some issues that can get overlooked in your decision to keep the house.

First, what is your house worth? Your tax bill may be of some help, as are websites like Zillow, but the only way to truly know the value of your home is to get an appraisal. Before you go to that expense, however, we suggest obtaining an Opinion of Value from a local, reputable real estate agent.

Once you know the value of the asset, subtract your mortgage and any lines of credit to find your equity. This is the amount you will need to "buy" from your spouse.

Mark and Alice came to meet with us. They're in their early 50's with 2 pre-teen children. Mark is a software engineer. Alice is now working part time after many years at home with the kids. They would like to keep the house so that their children can remain in the neighborhood schools with their friends.

Here's a snapshot of their assets:

Asset	Mark	Alice	Joint	
Real Property				
value: 600,000				
mtg: 325,000				
HELOC: 100,000				
Total Real Property			175,000	175,000
Non-Qualified Assets				
Brokerage Account		20,000		
Brokerage account	15,000			
Total Non-Qualified Assets	15,000	20,000		35,000
Qualified Assets				
401k	220,000			
Roth	65,000			
IRA		35,000		
Total Qualified Assets	285,000	35,000		320,000
TOTAL	300,000	55,000	175,000	530,000

Leaving out issues of selling costs and realtor's fees, here's what a straight 50/50 split of Mark and Alice's assets could look like:

Asset	Mark	Alice	Joint	
Real Property				
value: 600,000				
mtg: 325,000				
HELOC: 100,000				
Total Real Property	87,500	87,500		175,000
Non-Qualified Assets				
Brokerage Account	10,000	10,000		
Brokerage account	7,500	7,500		
Total Non-Qualified Assets	17,500	17,500		35,000
Qualified Assets				
401k	110,000	110,000		
Roth	32,500	32,500		
IRA	17,500	17,500		
Total Qualified Assets	160,000	160,000		320,000
TOTAL	265,000	265,000		530,000

Mark would like Alice to keep the house:

Asset	Mark	Alice	Joint	
Real Property				
value: 600,000				
mtg: 325,000				
HELOC: 100,000				
Total Real Property		175,000		175,000
Non-Qualified Assets				
Brokerage Account	10,000	10,000		
Brokerage account	7,500	7,500		
Total Non-Qualified Assets	17,500	17,500		35,000
Qualified Assets				
401k	215,000	5,000		
Roth	32,500	32,500		
IRA		35,000		
Total Qualified Assets	247,500	72,500		320,000
TOTAL	265,000	265,000		530,000

Alice would prefer that Mark keep the house:

Asset	Mark	Alice	Joint
Real Property			
value: 600,000	175,000		
mtg: 325,000			
HELOC: 100,000			
Total Real Property			175,000
Non-Qualified Assets			
Brokerage Account	10,000	10,000	
Brokerage account	7,500	7,500	
Total Non-Qualified Assets	17,500	17,500	35,000
Qualified Assets			
401k	40,000	175,000	
Roth	32,500	32,500	
IRA		35,000	
Total Qualified Assets	72,500	242,500	320,000
TOTAL	265,000	265,000	530,000

What are the issues for each of them?

If Mark takes the house:
- He gives up $87,500 from his retirement accounts to balance the assets.
- He takes on a $325,000 mortgage and a $100,000 home equity loan solely in his own name.

Mark has a good job and will be able to get a mortgage and is confident that the house will appreciate in the coming years. Even with child support, he can still contribute to his 401k going forward. Still, at the age of 53, he's concerned about the substantial impact on his retirement account.

If Alice takes the house:
- She gives up $87,500 in retirement assets that she would have been entitled to in the settlement.
- She takes on a $325,000 mortgage and a $100,000 home equity loan solely in her own name.
- She is working part time and her salary will not permit her to make any significant contributions to her retirement plan for the next 5 years.

The harsh reality is that even if she wants the house, she is not likely to qualify for a mortgage in her own name. Child support and alimony count as income for the purposes of obtaining a mortgage. However, most lenders require that the payments be in place for a period of one year before you apply.

The above brings us right back to the statement we made in our Introduction to this book: Your best strategy, before, during and after a divorce is knowledge- complete and thorough knowledge about your finances.

Mark and Alice completed their "to do" list as shown below. Together, we determined that selling the house would involve about 6% in costs (real estate commissions, legal fees, moving, etc.) and that after paying off the mortgage and HELOC each of them would net $69,500.

From speaking with a mortgage lender, Mark determined that he would be able to take his $69,500, use it as a down payment on a condo and qualify for a mortgage. He further determined that it might be preferable to qualify for the mortgage before he got divorced so that child support didn't count as a liability.

Alice determined that it would be at least a year before she would be eligible for a mortgage in her own name and she would need to rent in the interim. She spent several weekends looking at rentals. Rents in the area were higher than she anticipated. Knowing this led her to realize that without the proceeds from the sale of their current house she would have a difficult time covering her expenses.

A special note about "buying out your spouse."

In a divorce you may frequently hear the phrase "I bought my spouse out" when referring to the marital home. In fact, Renee used just those words in telling you the story about her house. But did she really "buy her spouse out" of the house? NO. She simply exchanged one asset she and her husband owned for another asset of equal value.

Let's look at a very simple example in a case where there are only 2 assets: a house and a retirement plan.

Asset	Mark	Jane	Joint	
Real Property				
value: 500,000			250,000	
mtg: 250,000				
Total Real Property	0	0	250,000	250,000
Retirement Assets				
Panda Corporation 401k	250,000			250,000
TOTAL	250,000	0	250,000	500,000

If the couple sells the house and divides both assets, leaving out closing costs, it would look like this:

Asset	Mark	Jane	Joint	
Real Property				
value: 500,000	125,000	125,000		
mtg: 250,000				
Total Real Property	125,0000	125,000		250,000
Retirement Assets				
Panda Corporation 401k	125,000	125,000		250,000
TOTAL	250,000	250,000	0	500,000

Instead, Jane decides to keep the house. Now the division of assets looks like this:

Asset	Mark	Jane	Joint	
Real Property				
value: 500,000		250,000		
mtg: 250,000				
Total Real Property	0	250,000		250,000
Retirement Assets				
Panda Corporation 401k	250,000			250,000
TOTAL	250,000	250,000		500,000

Now you can clearly see that Jane hasn't paid Mark anything for the house. She has exchanged her right to any 401k retirement assets for keeping the equity in the home.

Why is this important? Because, from a tax standpoint, Jane's basis stays exactly the same as it was when she and Mark first bought the house.

Let's say they bought it 20 years ago for $100,000. That's still Jane's basis. She doesn't add $125,000 to that for "buying Mark out" in the divorce.

Sometime later, Jane decides to sell:

    500,000   sale price
    100,000   (original purchase or basis)
    <u>30,000</u>   (closing costs)
    370,000   gain
    <u>250,000</u>   (exemption on sale of residence)
    120,000   taxable portion of house sale

Possible tax due: $18,000!

<u>Your To Do List</u>:

    1. Obtain an Opinion of Value.
    2. Talk with a mortgage lender, bank or credit union about your ability to obtain a mortgage.
    3. Go "shopping" in your neighborhood to look at alternative housing options such as rentals, condos or smaller homes.

Mistake #7: Failure to Understand the Rules of Retirement Accounts

Will You Still Need Me, Will You Still Feed Me...?

Acronyms, alphabet soup and numbers abound when talking about retirement plans: 401k, 403b, 457, IRA, ROTH, QDRO, RMD. How do you make sense of all of this when getting divorced?

First let's do a little basic review of the difference between a Traditional IRA and a Roth IRA.

A traditional IRA is money on which you HAVE NOT paid the taxes. You get a current year tax deduction on your income taxes for your contribution. The money grows tax deferred until you begin taking it out at age 70 ½ at which time you pay ordinary income taxes on the money you take out, not capital gains. One thing of great importance to note, there is a ten percent penalty tax for withdrawing money prior to age 59 ½. This means that IRA money is not money you should consider using for your daily living expenses, especially if you are not yet 59 ½. This account is considered funded with pre-tax money, as is a 401k, a 403b and a 457.

A Roth IRA is money on which you HAVE already paid taxes and you DO NOT get a current year income tax deduction. So I can already hear you asking "Renee and David, why would I want that?" And the answer is because money in a ROTH does not just grow tax deferred, it grows TAX FREE. We're going to repeat that, IT GROWS TAX FREE – FOREVER!!! Furthermore, there is no requirement that you ever take the money out. This account is considered funded with post-tax money.

Retirement assets and non-retirement assets are apples and oranges when considering an offset against each other in a divorce because of the tax implications. IRAs and ROTH IRAs, even though both retirement accounts, are also apples and oranges because of the tax implications.

All too often we see clients who decide to waive their right to a share of a retirement account in order to keep the marital home. Or, they take only retirement funds leaving themselves with no liquid (non-taxable) cash.

Let's look at a sample case to illustrate this:

Sarah is in her mid-60's. Her husband is in his late 60's.

Sarah came to us with the following assets:

Asset	Lester	Sarah	Joint	
Real Property				
Marital home	460,000			
Condo value: 675,000 mtg: 345,000		330,000		
Total Real Property				790,000
Non-Qualified Assets				
Bank Account	42,000			
Corporate stock	1,600			
Stock options	6,500			
Life insurance - cash value	105,000			
Cash		3,000		
Total Non-Qualified Assets	155,100	3,000		158,100
Qualified Assets				
IRA	110,800			
401k	653,400			
prior employer 401k	607,000			
IRA		130,000		
Total Qualified Assets	1,371,200	130,000		1,501,200
TOTAL	1,986,300	463,000		2,449,300

The proposal is for Lester to take the marital house and deal with all of the necessary repairs and costs associated with sale. Sarah will keep the condo as her residence. In order to accomplish this, Sarah is given a larger share of the 401(k).

Asset	Lester	Sarah	Joint	
Real Property				
Marital home	460,000			
Condo value: 675,000 mtg: 345,000		330,000		
Total Real Property				790,000
Non-Qualified Assets				
Bank Account	21,000	21,000		
Corporate stock	800	800		
Stock options	3,250	3,250		
Life insurance - cash value	105,000			
Cash		3,000		
Total Non-Qualified Assets	130,050	28,050		158,100
Qualified Assets				
IRA	55,400	55,400		
401k	326,700	326,700		
prior employer 401k	252,000	355,000		
IRA		130,000		
Total Qualified Assets	634,100	867,100		1,501,200
TOTAL	1,224,150	1,225,150		2,449,300

What are the issues?

In reviewing this case, we note that Lester gets the marital home tax free. There are no capital gains issues, therefore no taxes will be due. If we subtract 6% for closing costs, Lester realizes $432,400 in tax free cash. Sarah, by contrast, will pay at least 15% in income taxes on a similar amount of IRA money. Looking at this proposal, Sarah has no liquid, non-taxable assets. She will be depending on her IRA and social security as her income source. One option is to give Sarah the IRA money plus an additional 15% (115%) to offset the taxes.

A preferable option is to divide the marital home upon sale. Sarah can use her share to reduce her mortgage, or to pay her mortgage monthly. This allows her to draw less from her IRA annually for her living expenses in excess of the RMD thereby reducing her taxes.

Asset	Lester	Sarah	Joint	
Real Property				
Marital home	~~460,000~~			
Condo		330,000		
value: 675,000				
mtg: 345,000				
Total Real Property				330,000
Non-Qualified Assets				
Marital Home sold	230,000	230,000		
Bank Account	21,000	21,000		
Corporate stock	800	800		
Stock options	3,250	3,250		
Life insurance - cash value	105,000			
Cash		3,000		
Total Non-Qualified Assets	360,050	258,050		618,100
Qualified Assets				
IRA	110,800			
401k	326,700	326,700		
prior employer 401k	362,000	245,000		
IRA	65,000	65,000		
Total Qualified Assets	864,500	636,700		1,501,200
TOTAL	1,224,50	1,224,750		2,449,300

Dividing Assets in Retirement Accounts- A Short How-to Guide

Traditional IRA and Roth IRA
It's relatively easy to divide money in an IRA or a ROTH. The divorce decree will specify the account to be divided. Along with the forms requested by the bank, brokerage firm or investment company, this will usually suffice to allow the transfer of IRA funds to a new account for the other spouse.

Note that if you are getting funds from your former spouse's IRA, it will be your ex-spouse who will be responsible for getting the forms completed. We suggest that you call the custodian of the IRA and find out specifically what forms will be required, obtain the blank forms and have them available for your ex to complete.

401(k)
Assets held in a 401(k), however, are a bit more complex. These require a Qualified Domestic Relations Order (QDRO) to make the transfer. The realm of QDRO law is vast and complex and beyond the scope of this book. Our objective is to make you aware of a few facts surrounding the process:

1. you will need a QDRO specialist, usually an attorney, to draft the document
2. it governs assets in a 401k plan or a 403(b) plan
3. there is no time frame for filing the QDRO
4. if you are under 59½ you may be able to avoid the 10% penalty for early withdrawal

Let's take each of the above issues:

1. You will need a QDRO specialist, usually an attorney, to draft the document – your attorney will either do this or recommend someone who can draft the document. Once drafted it goes to the judge and the retirement plan administrator for approval. The purpose of the QDRO is to instruct the retirement plan administrator to create a separate account for the ex-spouse.

2. Assets in a corporate retirement account are covered by a QDRO. What happens if you have assets in a 401k from a prior job? Remember Sarah and Lester from the examples above?

Asset	Lester	Sarah	Joint	
Qualified Assets				
IRA	110,800			
401k	653,400			
prior employer 401k	607,000			
IRA		130,000		
Total Qualified Assets	1,371,200	130,000		1,501,200
TOTAL	1,986,300	463,000		2,449,300

Lester can roll the assets in his old 401k into an IRA solely in his own name. Once in an IRA it can be divided without a QDRO. That leaves this couple with only one QDRO needed for the current 401k and a slightly lower legal bill.

3. QDRO's can be filed at any time but DO NOT delay. We have seen clients 5 years post-divorce who still have not transferred assets in a 401k plan. If your ex-spouse dies, retires, changes jobs and the QDRO is not filed, you may have little recourse to collect assets that are due to you.

4. As with an IRA, you can avoid taxes by making a custodian to custodian transfer directly from the 401k plan custodian to your new IRA. If you have them send you a check, they will automatically withhold 20% for taxes. For example, if you are awarded a $100,000 distribution from your ex-spouse's 401(k) you will actually receive only $80,000. If you are under 59 ½ you will also owe a 10% penalty.

Let's look at an actual example of how this transfer works for another couple:

- Carol, age 55, and Steve, age 60, are going through a divorce. What is important here? Carol is under the age 59 ½ requirement for being able to withdraw funds from a retirement account without a 10% penalty.

- Steve has $560,000 in his 401(k) that will be divided by a QDRO, transferring $280,000 to Carol.

- Carol can transfer the money directly to her IRA. She will pay no taxes until she starts withdrawing funds after age 59 1/2, at which time she would pay ordinary income tax on the amount withdrawn.

- But Carol needs $80,000 for a down payment on a condo. So she holds back $100,000 *before* transferring the remaining amount to her IRA. 20% is withheld for taxes, leaving her with $80,000 to spend without incurring a 10% penalty.

- Once she transfers the remaining $180,000 to her IRA, the 59 ½ rule applies to the remainder of the money. Six months later, Carol realizes that she needs another $10,000 to buy a car. Now, she will have to pay the 10% penalty and the taxes on that money. If she had thought of it earlier, she could have taken $112,500 from the 401(k) before the transfer to give herself $90,000 without the penalty.

As noted above, IRA's do not require a QDRO to divide the assets. Also, there is no 20% mandatory tax withholding on a transfer. To avoid paying taxes, you must deposit any distribution from an IRA directly to your own IRA, existing or newly established. This is called a custodian to custodian transfer. If a check is sent to you, you must deposit the money into your own IRA within 60 days to avoid a taxable distribution.

A Note about Social Security

Finally, some good news about divorce. If your marriage lasted at least ten years, you can claim social security benefits on the entire earnings history of your ex-spouse. This is true even if you have never worked.

You can receive benefits on your ex-spouse's record if:

- You are unmarried;
- You are age 62 or older;
- Your ex-spouse is entitled to Social Security retirement or disability benefits and
- The benefit you are entitled to receive based on your own work is less than the benefit you would receive based on your ex-spouse's work.

You are entitled to claim one-half of your ex-spouse's benefits or all of your own benefits, whichever is greater. Collecting on your former spouse's benefits doesn't reduce what your ex-spouse receives, or, if he's remarried, what his current spouse receives.

Because this is a legal right to which you are entitled, and is not negotiable during a divorce, social security is often not considered when looking at the division of assets. This is a mistake because social security can have a significant impact on retirement, especially for a woman who was out of the workforce for many years raising children.

When you are ready to claim social security benefits, be sure to let the Social Security Administration know that you were married for more than ten years, and be prepared to furnish your ex-spouse's full name and social security number.

They will then calculate what benefits will give you the highest monthly payment, and they will be able to recalculate those benefits if your ex-spouse dies while you are collecting benefits.

Your To Do List:

1. Don't give up all the non-taxable cash in your settlement for an equal amount of retirement money.
2. Understand the tax ramifications of withdrawing money from retirement accounts.
3. Go to www.ssa.gov to get an estimate of your Social Security retirement benefits.

Mistake #8: Not Maintaining Control over Insurance Policies

Who's Got You Covered?

Many people going through a divorce have often uttered the words "it would be so much easier if he, or she, had just died." While this is an understandable sentiment, think about the reality of the financial impact this would have. Your spouse owes you alimony. How do you collect?

Most divorce decrees call for one, or both, of the parties to obtain a life insurance policy to insure the value of alimony payments, child support or some other financial need. One day, this unfortunate event does come to pass. Remembering your divorce decree, you quickly call the insurance company. Much to your surprise, you learn that the life insurance policy lapsed years ago for non-payment of the premium.

What could you have done?

If you are the person for whom the insurance is obtained, you can be:
- the owner of the policy
- irrevocable beneficiary of the policy
- receive notice from the company if the premiums are not being paid

Without some arrangement, the ex-spouse who took out the policy could easily stop making payments and you would never know about it until the policy is needed and it no longer exists. This could be financially devastating. As the owner or irrevocable beneficiary, you would be notified of any outstanding issues with the policy, such as non-payment of the premium, and could therefore take action and prevent the policy from lapsing or being cancelled.

If insurance needs to be applied for and put in place, please make certain to obtain it <u>before</u> you get divorced. One client agreed to obtain insurance and then, post-divorce, learned that he was not insurable. The divorce had already been granted and the assets divided. This necessitated many meetings with the attorneys and additional legal expenses that could have been avoided.

What if you or your spouse is not insurable?

Non-insurability may be a matter of health or concern about being rated. It may also be a matter of the cost of the premium if you're getting divorced late in life.

Depending on the amount of insurance needed, and the assets in the family, alternatives can be:
- the purchase of an annuity with a death benefit
- retaining the ex-spouse as the beneficiary on an IRA

Note that this solution has tax consequences that life insurance does not. Still, if insurance is not an option, an annuity or IRA may be a viable alternative.

Health insurance can be another fallout in a divorce. Typically one party carries the health insurance for the entire family. What happens after the divorce? Certainly the children remain covered in any family policy. But, do you as the ex-spouse have the right to continued coverage?

The answer is <u>That Depends</u>.

If you or your spouse works for a Massachusetts employer and you have family coverage then it is highly likely that the divorced spouse will be entitled to continuing health benefits at no additional cost until one of you remarries.

As good as that sounds, there are many exceptions to the rule including these common ones:
- You or your spouse works for a company that self-insures or is self-funded
- You or your spouse works for an out-of-state company
- You or your spouse changes jobs after the divorce.

Renee: When I got divorced I was self-employed and my husband carried the health insurance for our family. A family plan cost the same whether we were two, three, four or eight on the policy. My ex, the kids and I stayed on the family plan for many years until one day my ex-spouse remarried. His company HR administrator called to tell me that my ex-husband's new wife was now on the family plan with him and my kids and I was off! I panicked, called several attorney friends, dug out my divorce agreement, finally took a deep breath and called the insurance company. Much to my relief I found that I was entitled to a policy in my own name under the company umbrella at the group rate although I would have to pay for it myself.

Before your divorce is finalized, determine what type of insurance you or your spouse has. Is it private, insured or self-insured? Is it through a government employer or the military? Do not take your spouse's word for it that you may continue on the plan. Get confirmation directly from the company. Obtain a copy of the "Summary Plan Description" from the employer and study it carefully or consult an experienced lawyer. Ask the company if there is specific language you can include in your divorce agreement that will require them to cover you?

If you determine that coverage is not available research other options and the cost so you can negotiate payment for health insurance as part of your settlement. COBRA, although expensive, will be available to you for 36 months in a divorce.

Your To Do List:

    1. Determine how your health insurance coverage will be provided
    2. Should you or your spouse get life insurance to protect child support and/or alimony obligations?

Mistake #9: Failure to Update Estate Documents

Die and Endow a College or a Cat... but Not Your Ex-Spouse
(With apologies to Alexander Pope)

Somewhere early on in the pages of your divorce agreement will be a paragraph similar to this:

<u>Waiver of Estate Claims</u>
The parties each hereby waive any right they may have at law or in equity to take under any Last Will and Testament made by the other, including all rights of dower, curtsey, or statutory allowance....

What you have done is agreed that each of you may no longer inherit from the other with respect to assets that pass by will or by the laws of intestacy in your state.

There are however many assets that pass via contractual agreement. Among these are IRA's, life insurance, annuities and 401(k) assets.

After a divorce, many people forget to change the beneficiaries on their life insurance policies and individual retirement accounts and may not update their wills. The noted case in this matter was decided by the U.S. Supreme Court in 2009: <u>Kennedy vs the Plan Administrator for the DuPont Savings and Investment Plan</u>.

While married, William Kennedy had named his wife Liv Kennedy as his beneficiary. Years later, in the divorce decree, she waived her rights to any benefits under his retirement plans.

When William Kennedy died, he hadn't changed his beneficiary designation in the plan. His daughter maintained that there was no named beneficiary on the account since Liv had waived her rights in the divorce decree. But DuPont said its only option was to follow the beneficiary designation form which listed Liv Kennedy.

The Kennedy estate sued DuPont and the plan administrator for the funds. After years of wending its way through the courts, the case finally went to the US Supreme Court which unanimously ruled that the person named on the beneficiary form gets the money.

Don't let a court case decide the disposition of your estate. Call all of the companies where you have assets and request Change of Beneficiary forms. Complete them but do not sign or date until after the divorce. Once your divorce is finalized, sign and date the forms, mail to the respective companies and request confirmation of receipt of the beneficiary changes for your records.

Under certain circumstances, you may be leaving your ex-spouse assets. If this is the case, redo the beneficiary forms so that they are dated post-divorce and your intent is clear. This will avoid any unnecessary conflict later on.

What if you have minor children?

Your ex-spouse is still your child's parent and will become the legal guardian of any funds you leave to your child. If that idea causes you distress, consider setting up a Testamentary Trust or a Living Trust for your assets. This will allow you to name someone other than your ex-spouse as the custodian of any funds you leave to your children upon your death.

Your To Do List:

1. Redo your will
2. Consider a trust
3. Redo your living will or health care proxy
4. Redo your durable power of attorney
5. Change all beneficiaries on IRAs, 401(k) plans, annuities and life insurance policies

Mistake #10: Failure to Follow Through Once the Divorce is Final

It Ain't Over 'til It's Over

The decree is signed, you've gone before the Judge, and the nisi period has passed. *Is it over yet?*

Legally, yes. However, the paper work and the follow up is not.

Is there property to be transferred? Are there bank accounts to be divided? Do you need to QDRO a 401k?

Whose responsibility is it to make sure that all of the assets divided pursuant to your divorce are retitled and in what time frame is this to occur?

Lots of questions.

Our suggestion is that you have a post-divorce "To Do" list. We've included a "to do" list after each previous chapter, so if you've already done all those items, you're probably in decent shape. Even so, there are several items that often fall through the cracks.

Here is a partial list of some of things that might be on it:

1. Prepare and record deed(s) to transfer title to all real estate

2. Refinance mortgages to all real estate in accordance with the new ownership and make certain old mortgages are discharged

3. Transfer title to motor vehicles and refinance/reinsure as needed

4. Change the beneficiaries on all annuities, retirement accounts, life insurance and pensions

5. Contact banks and brokerage firms holding non retirement accounts for paperwork to transfer ownership or divide accounts

6. Contact the custodian of your IRA and ROTH accounts to acquire the paperwork to transfer proceeds to your ex-spouse (or vice versa). Do not accept a check made payable directly to you which may have tax consequences. A custodian to custodian transfer is tax free.

7. Divide any pensions or 401k plans with a QDRO. This can be a lengthy process so do not let it linger too long after the divorce.

Equally as important as what you need to do is that you designate the party, or parties, that will be responsible for each item: you, your ex, your attorney or your ex-spouse's attorney. Then target a completion date for each item. It is all too easy to find that months, sometimes years, go by and that assets have not been transferred, deeds have not been recorded and the QDRO is still not done.

Keep your "To Do" list handy and update it regularly.

Conclusion

We hope you found this book helpful as you work through what may be the most difficult time of your life.

While it would be impossible to discuss every situation that could occur in a divorce, we have focused on the mistakes that we see people make most often. It's not unusual in a divorce for one spouse to be more "financially-savvy" than the other. In those cases, it's easy to see how the less financially-savvy spouse can be taken advantage of. Knowledge and an understanding of the process and some key financial concepts can help level the playing field.

We hope you'll be able to look back someday and remember this time as the beginning of your new life- not just the end of your old one. You're getting divorced for a reason, whether it was your decision or not. Taking the proper steps early in your divorce process can help get your new life off to a happy and financially-secure start.

We hope your divorce is as amicable and painless as possible and we wish you a lifetime of happiness moving forward.

Contacting Renee and David

Senes & Chwalek Financial Advisors is located outside of Boston and serves clients throughout Massachusetts.

For more information, please visit our website www.senesandchwalek.com.

Made in the USA
Middletown, DE
19 September 2017